Sandy's Tea Society

Delighting in Friendships Steeped in Love

Paintings and Text by

SANDY LYNAM CLOUGH

HARVEST HOUSE PUBLISHERS
EUGENE, OREGON 97402

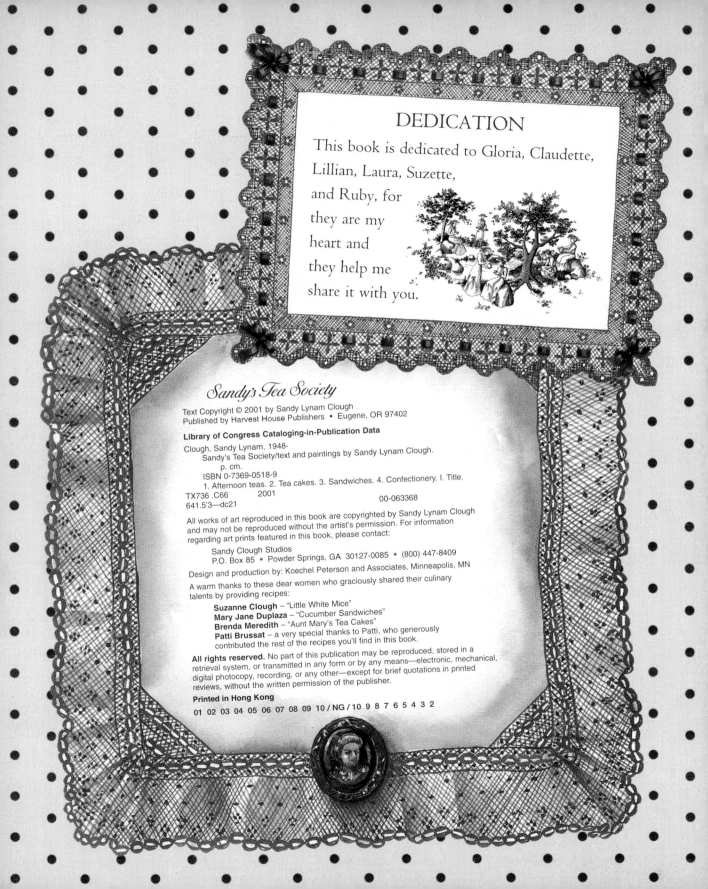

DEDICATION

This book is dedicated to Gloria, Claudette, Lillian, Laura, Suzette, and Ruby, for they are my heart and they help me share it with you.

Sandy's Tea Society

Text Copyright © 2001 by Sandy Lynam Clough
Published by Harvest House Publishers • Eugene, OR 97402

Library of Congress Cataloging-in-Publication Data

Clough, Sandy Lynam, 1948-
  Sandy's Tea Society/text and paintings by Sandy Lynam Clough.
    p. cm.
  ISBN 0-7369-0518-9
  1. Afternoon teas. 2. Tea cakes. 3. Sandwiches. 4. Confectionery. I. Title.
TX736 .C66   2001
641.5'3—dc21   00-063368

Sandy Clough Studios
    P.O. Box 85 • Powder Springs, GA 30127-0085 • (800) 447-8409

Design and production by: Koechel Peterson and Associates, Minneapolis, MN

A warm thanks to these dear women who graciously shared their culinary talents by providing recipes:

Suzanne Clough – "Little White Mice"
Mary Jane Duplaza – "Cucumber Sandwiches"
Brenda Meredith – "Aunt Mary's Tea Cakes"
Patti Brussat – a very special thanks to Patti, who generously contributed the rest of the recipes you'll find in this book.

Printed in Hong Kong

01 02 03 04 05 06 07 08 09 10 / NG / 10 9 8 7 6 5 4 3 2

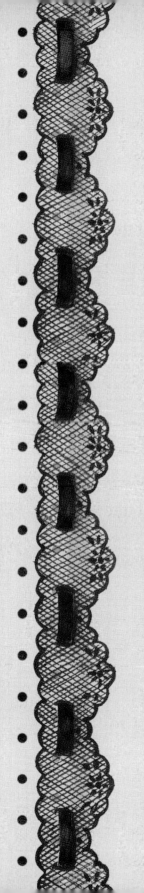

Contents

In Sandy's Tearoom

WELCOME TO MY TEAROOM! WON'T you come in and join us? Please don't hesitate just because you don't know anyone else here. Although they are all favorite friends of mine, these ladies do not know each other either, and that is precisely why they are here!

I have invited these special ladies to tea because they have one thing in common: They are very rich. Oh, they're not wealthy financially. But they *are* truly rich because in their hearts is a wealth of warmth and caring and individual style and creativity, all just waiting to be shared. And yet each lady also has a need. She needs good friends. She wants to be part of a group of friends who are kindred hearts, but she is not sure how to develop these true friendships.

May I present my friends Laura, Ruby, Claudette, Lillian, Gloria, and Suzette? They are all very different from each other, yet perhaps not so different from you.

Now that I have poured the tea and made sure everyone has been served cucumber sandwiches, cookies, and petits fours, it is time to interrupt the tinkling of silver spoons and teacups to make introductions. I have asked each lady to introduce herself and to share some of her special interests.

Lillian, who is as delicate as her name sounds, volunteers to go first. "Well," she says with a smile, "my mother should have named me 'Rose,' because I love the romance of roses. My garden is filled with roses, and the fabrics and wallpaper in my home are covered with cabbage roses. None of my china matches, but every single piece has roses on it. And, oh, I almost forgot! I love to sew and help other people make things."

Tenderhearted Claudette speaks up next. "I love collecting antiques and well-loved things, like old lace and delicate vintage teacups. Cracks and little chips don't bother me—they are symbols of survival. They remind me to be fragile, yet strong."

"I'm just a country girl at heart," joins in Suzette, "and a gardener. I grow many varieties of flowers in my cottage garden, but I especially love daisies. I'm always looking for colorful floral handkerchiefs like the ones my mother used to carry, and I have a drawer full of vintage aprons."

Ruby, an artist whose ideas are her stock-in-trade, pipes up next. "Using my creativity is such a joy for me. The whole world is a feast for my eyes. My problem is, I can think of more things to make and do than I could ever have time for!"

Gloria is next to share her interests. "I love the outdoors! Croquet is my favorite game." She pauses with a twinkle in her eye. "In fact, I usually beat the gentlemen! I enjoy walking in the woods among the ferns and wildflowers, but I do not like snakes!"

We all laugh in agreement and turn to Laura, the quiet one. She is so unassuming that she is unaware of her own elegance.

Laura always prefers to listen to others and not talk about herself. But she is quite ready to share her love of both reading and writing with this group. "Books have always been my silent friends," she confides.

What a delightfully different group of friends I have brought together! And yet the whole group has such a dear romantic flavor. It's obvious to me that they are kindred hearts. I can hardly wait to explain my idea to them.

"I have invited you all here today not just for tea but also for encouragement," I begin. "I want to encourage you to form your own ladies' tea society so that you can build friendships together as you make memories and share creative ideas around the warmth of taking tea."

"How can we do that?" asks Suzette.

"Just by meeting together for tea. Each of you can take a turn hosting a special tea party in your home," I reply.

"Oh, let's do!" comes a chorus of voices. Right then and there, they agree not to try to impress each other with their decor or cleverness, but to truly serve one another in kindness as they share the delights of their own individuality and creativity.

Laura quickly composes a motto for the new tea society: "Joining kindred hearts with a cup of friendship." Because I have brought them together, they surprise me by calling themselves "Sandy's Tea Society."

Although I have helped them to get started with a few creative ideas and recipes, these ladies are brimming with their own ideas for tea parties—ideas that can only originate in generous, sharing hearts.

You and I have been invited to visit these very special—and original—tea parties. Not only will the ladies wear the vintage fashions we all sometimes wish we could wear, they will also share with us their ideas for decorating and setting their tea tables, graciously entertaining, developing friendships, and preparing special recipes.

Won't you please join us for tea?

Sandy Lynam Clough

Claudette's Tea

VERY CAREFULLY, CLAUDETTE LIFTED six teacups and six saucers out of her cupboard and gingerly placed them upon her lace-covered dining room table. She was filled with anticipation. Never before had she served tea in these cups. Claudette was content to sip her own tea from the antique teacups she had collected. Those cups had cracks and even little chips in  them. But these teacups were special. These teacups had been her mother's. Although she herself had never filled these cups with tea, Claudette knew that they were filled with her own memories of her mother's tea parties. The rustle of silk taffeta dresses, the aroma of hot scones, her mother's gracious hospitality— all her happy memories of helping her mother pour tea were stored in these six cups.

Almost before she could think about it, Claudette had volunteered to host the first tea party for this brand-new tea society. She was so eager to use her teacups!

As she arranged soft globes of ivory hydrangea blossoms in an old silver teapot that had lost its lid, she was pleased to note that her table was already taking on a soft elegance. Although she loved the beauty of a formal tea, Claudette didn't want this party to be too formal, so she had sent the following invitation to her new friends:

It's a joy to be your hostess,
I'm as honored as can be
To ask you to please join me
For a vintage fashion tea.

Join me as we celebrate
A bygone era's charm,

Add a brooch, a shawl, or a boa
Draped across your arm.

An antique dress, a drawstring purse
We'd love to see all that—
Express your style and femininity,
Just please don't wear a hat!

Claudette was certain that a vintage fashion theme would keep conversation flowing for the society's first tea. Besides, dressing up was downright fun!

The doorbell chimed just as Claudette was glancing in the mirror and straightening the cameo brooch that fastened her lace cape. She opened the door and welcomed Suzette, Lillian, Gloria, Ruby, and Laura, who presented her with a hostess gift from all of them. Claudette was deeply touched by her new friends' thoughtfulness. Knowing how she loved old things, they had given her an antique silver demitasse spoon, thinking (correctly!) that she might enjoy collecting them. Thanking them one by one, Claudette ushered her guests into her living room, where she had set up folding tables.

Now the ladies knew why Claudette had said not to wear a hat! For on the tables, there sat everything they needed to make

their own beautiful hats for their first tea. What fun!

When the last hat was finished, the ladies put them on and had an impromptu fashion show. Laura was attired in her mother's wedding dress, Suzette wore a lovely eyelet summer frock, and Gloria modeled a simple evening gown her mother had worn to her first dance. Lillian didn't own any vintage

CLAUDETTE'S HATS

To give her guests the chance to create their own hats, Claudette purchased inexpensive, wide-brimmed straw hats, silk flowers, artificial fruit, feathers, yards of tulle, and lots of ribbon. To encourage conversation, she only set out two glue guns and two pairs of scissors. Having to share would encourage her new friends to talk! She needn't have worried about that—before the glue was dry, they were all laughing and talking together like old friends.

clothing, so she had made herself a beautiful black brocade vest. She added a "collar" by attaching half of an antique hankie on each side of the neck open-ing. She then added vintage buttons and attached an antique charm bracelet where a watch chain might be. Ruby had created a "vintage" blouse by transferring locket-sized old photos onto fabric and then covering buttons with the fabric. How wonderful each of the ladies looked in her fashionable attire!

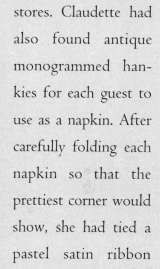

After the spirited conversation and fashion show, the ladies entered the dining room as Claudette brought the food out from the kitchen. There they were transported from the world of vintage fashion to the grace of yesteryear. The table's crowning joy was a cake shaped like a hat that was perched on a glass cake stand. Around the base of the hat's crown were pansies freshly picked from Claudette's window box. A big bow of French ribbon adorned one side of the cake. Around the base of the cake stand were

small, framed pictures of vintage fashions, which had been collected from the fashion magazines Claudette had found at antique stores. Claudette had also found antique monogrammed han-kies for each guest to use as a napkin. After carefully folding each napkin so that the prettiest corner would show, she had tied a pastel satin ribbon around the middle as a napkin ring, then fastened the bow with an old pin or earring.

Beside each plate Claudette had tucked an old pair of gloves. Her guests were invited to take these, as well as the hankies, home with them. The ladies hurried to try on these fancy gloves before the tea was served.

Each place setting was highlighted by a one-of-a-kind teacup that had belonged to Claudette's mother. Thin cheese straws (which Claudette called "hat pins"), ribbon sandwiches, and sugar scones were arranged on beautiful pieces of vintage china. Because none of the china matched, each setting was a distinctly beautiful presentation. In little

Sandy Lynam Clough

porcelain baskets sat orange marmalade and a new version of Devonshire cream, which was promptly named "Sandy's Tea Society Cream." Not only was it delicious, it was also so easy to make that everyone wanted to include it at her own tea! "Buttons"—sugar cookies decorated like buttons with borders, stripes, and polka dots of icing—rested on a lacy paper doily in an antique silver Victorian cake basket.

Claudette poured Earl Grey tea from an old Bavarian teapot decorated with rows of pansies and offered sugar cubes, cream, and lemon slices to her friends as they served themselves from her beautiful table. After they were all seated, Claudette asked each guest to tell about the most memorable dress she had ever owned. As they reminisced about ball gowns, Easter frocks, and back-to-school dresses, the memories turned to favorite places and special people. Exchanging stories, it became apparent they had all been influenced by their mothers' fashion tastes. Gloria pointed out that her wedding dress would be her most memorable dress—if only she had a reason to buy one!

All too soon, the delightful afternoon was over. As the tea society bid each other fond good-byes, Gloria admonished everyone to hold onto their hats—they would need them again soon. But Laura's turn to host the tea came next. Claudette had surprised them all. They couldn't help but wonder what Laura had in store for them!

CLAUDETTE'S GLOVES

For her one-of-a-kind take-home favors,
Claudette made "vintage" gloves for each guest.
Having accumulated these gloves here and
there at thrift shops, she embellished them
with a row of pearls on the edge (using pearls
"by the yard" from the fabric department),
a ruffle of lace, or an old rhinestone
bracelet sewn on. Each lady was duly
impressed with her fine new accessory!

Claudette's
TEA MENU

Ribbon Sandwiches

Hat Pins (Cheese Straws)

*Sugar Scones with Sandy's
Tea Society Cream*

Fashion Hat Cake

"Button" Cookies

Earl Grey Tea

HAT PINS (CHEESE STRAWS)

1 pound sharp cheddar cheese, grated
½ tsp salt • 1¾ cups all-purpose flour
½ cup butter, creamed • ¼ tsp red pepper flakes

In a large bowl, combine all of the
ingredients and mix well. Refrigerate
for 1 hour. Roll into a thin rectangle
and cut into narrow strips 4 inches
long. Bake at 350 degrees for 20-25 minutes.

RIBBON SANDWICHES

1 loaf unsliced white bread
1 loaf unsliced wheat bread
1 8-ounce can tuna, drained
¼ cup minced celery
1 tblsp sweet pickle, chopped
4 hard-boiled eggs
½ cup mayonnaise • 1 tsp mustard
dash of salt • dash of pepper

Shell and chop eggs, then mix with ¼ cup mayonnaise, mustard, salt, and pepper. Drain tuna, then mix with ¼ cup mayonnaise, celery, and sweet pickle. Refrigerate each mixture in a separate bowl. Trim crusts from each loaf of bread. Slice each loaf into 5-7 horizontal slices. Alternating white with wheat bread, spread tuna and egg mixtures on each horizontal slice. Wrap loaf in foil or plastic wrap and refrigerate overnight. Cut loaf of alternating bread and fillings into 15-20 crosswise slices. (Each slice can be halved.) Keep refrigerated until ready to serve.

"BUTTON" COOKIES

refrigerated roll of sugar cookie dough
tubes of colored icing • straws

Reshape the roll of cookie dough into a round tube if it has become flattened on the bottom. Thinly slice unbaked cookies. Using a straw, cut two side-by-side holes near the center of each cookie to *mimic* the holes in buttons. Bake according to package directions. After cookies are cooled, decorate with icing, creating polka dots, stripes, and a circle around the edge.

SUGAR SCONES

2 cups flour
1 tsp baking powder
¼ cup butter
1 tsp vanilla
5 tsp sugar • ⅔ cup milk

Preheat oven to 425 degrees. Dust a baking sheet with flour. Sift flour and baking powder into a mixing bowl, then stir to mix. Add butter, then stir in sugar. Make a well in the center of the dry mixture. Add milk, mixing it in until dough is soft but not sticky. Turn out dough onto a floured surface and knead lightly. Pat dough out to one-inch thick. Using a round cookie cutter, cut out 12 scones. Arrange on floured baking sheet and dust the tops of the scones with flour. Bake 12 minutes or until lightly browned. Serve with butter or jam.

SANDY'S TEA SOCIETY CREAM

½ cup sour cream
½ cup Cool Whip

Stir ingredients together. Serve chilled.

FASHION HAT CAKE

Claudette made her hat cake with a cake mix and ready-to-use frosting that she tinted pale yellow with a bit of food coloring. She used a large skillet the size of her cake stand to bake a layer that would be the brim. She baked the "crown" in a small stainless steel mixing bowl.

Sandy Lynam Clough

Laura's Tea

AS SHE BACKED INTO HER FRONT doorway, Laura shook the rain off her umbrella. She couldn't wait to slip off her soggy shoes and place them on the hearth to dry. Although it was spring, it was still early in the season, and the chill and dampness only made the clouds seem gloomier. Laura shut the door on the dreary day. Although it was gloomy outside, there was no gloom in her heart—only happiness! The weather gave her a perfect chance to prepare a cozy tea for her new friends in front of the cheery fire in her living room. She had invited the tea society to her home for a four o'clock afternoon tea.

Laura had already put her small kitchen table in front of the fireplace and surrounded it with six chairs. A floor-length tapestry cloth was topped by a beautiful white cutwork

tablecloth. Laura had chosen the elegance of white china with a simple gold trim for her tea. Quite fond of what are called "head vases," she had accumulated enough to decorate her table. A head vase is the head and shoulders of a beautiful lady dressed up with earrings, pearls, and a hat. The hat has no top so that the vase can be filled with flowers, giving the effect of an exuberant hat of lovely flowers on a lady out to tea. Laura chose her six favorite vases and filled them with spring flowers from the market. She sat each one on a round crocheted doily. They looked to all the world like a committee formed to promote the advancement of spring and to forecast sunny skies!

Instead of using place cards, Laura had selected a heartfelt sentiment for each of her guests from her collection of antique autograph books. For each lady, she had purchased a pretty journal as a gift. On the first

page, she wrote the friend's name and the sentiment she had chosen from an old autograph book. For Suzette, she had found:

> *Flowers will fade away,*
> *And they will soon decay,*
> *Let not our friendship fade so fast*
> *But let it forever last.*

This one seemed as though it were written for Lillian, even though it was dated 1890:

> *Sweet as fragrant roses*
> *It is to have a friend.*
> *On whom in storm or sunshine*
> *You know you can depend.*

For Ruby, she wrote from an 1889 inscription:

> *Accept, dear Ruby, my wish sincere—*
> *May every bliss attend you,*
> *May this one be a happy year*
> *And angels kind befriend you.*

She had found similar fitting sentiments for the rest of her friends. She would place the journals on little easels at all of their places before the ladies arrived.

After Claudette's tea, Laura already considered these ladies to be friends and not just acquaintances. She was truly interested in them and what was important to them, and she wanted to be a friend they could count on.

Laura had been to teas where the polite question was, "How are you?" and the standard answer was "Fine, thank you." The answer was always the same, no matter if the inquiry was "How has your day been?" or "How is your family?" "Fine." Always "fine."

"It's impossible," she thought to herself, "to weep with those who weep and rejoice with those who rejoice if everything is always 'fine.'"

Laura was too polite and too kind to put her friends on the spot with prying questions, but she did want to let the spotlight shine on them. She wanted to draw attention to their hearts, interests, and accomplishments.

After she put the finishing touches on the food for the tea, she placed little scrolls tied with ribbon on the saucers of the teacups. She lit the candles in the center of the table and opened the journals so that the ladies could see their names. Just then the doorbell chimed as if to say, "We're here!"

Laura welcomed her friends into the house, helping them with their coats, cloaks, and umbrellas. Then she quickly ushered them into the warmth of her cheery, cozy living room with its dark red Oriental rug and shelves filled with favorite books and photographs.

When the ladies had found their places and were seated, Laura served them hot chicken pillows, apple cake, spiced peach muffins, and caramelized Bosc pears. The simplicity of white paper doilies on white china showcased the warm, comforting teatime spread that Laura had prepared. Fragrant orange spice tea filled their cups in an arched stream from the teapot. The food was so inviting! But no one took a bite until her hostess

Sandy Lynum Clough

had finished serving and had settled herself at the table. After Laura had taken the first bite of food and sip of tea, the others joined in.

"Please," said Lillian, "tell us about the scrolls!"

"Well," replied Laura, "you may open yours and see what it says."

"It's a question!"

"Yes," said Laura, "they are all questions." And then silently to herself: *Questions that can't be answered with the word "fine."* "We can all take turns answering them."

"Mine asks, 'What is your favorite memory?'" Lillian didn't have to think long. "It is of my mother teaching me how to properly hold a needle and how to embroider. Her patience and love for needlework helped me learn those same skills, as well as the joy of creativity. We have spent so many happy hours stitching and talking together."

 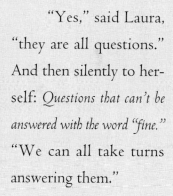

Laura's
TEA MENU

Hot Chicken Pillows

Apple Cake

Spiced Peach Muffins

Caramelized Bosc Pears

Orange Spice Tea

CARAMELIZED BOSC PEARS

2 ripe pears • 2 tblsps brown sugar
1 ½ tblsps salted butter, melted

Preheat broiler. Halve pears lengthwise, then scoop out core and seeds with melon corer. Arrange pears cut side up in a small baking dish. Brush with butter, then sprinkle hollow in middle with brown sugar. Broil pears 4 inches from heat for 8 minutes or until sugar caramelizes.

APPLE CAKE

2 cups whole wheat flour • 1 cup sugar • ¼ cup toasted wheat germ

1 cup brown sugar • 1 tsp cinnamon • 1 cup chopped walnuts

1 tsp salt • 2 eggs, beaten • ½ tsp nutmeg

1 tsp vanilla • 4 cups diced apple • ½ cup oil • 2 tsps baking soda

Preheat oven to 350 degrees. Sift together whole wheat flour, wheat germ, baking soda, cinnamon, salt, and nutmeg. Set aside. In a large bowl, combine peeled and diced apples, sugars, oil, walnuts, eggs, and vanilla. Add flour to mixture. Stir gently, blending well. Turn into a 2" deep pan. Bake at 350 degrees for 50 minutes or until cake pulls easily from side of pan. Cool in pan or on rack. Sprinkle with confectioner's sugar, if desired. Cut into 12 bars.

HOT CHICKEN PILLOWS

1 cup dried cranberries • 1 tblsp butter

1 cup diced celery • 1 cup diced apple

1½ cups cooked, diced chicken • 1 cup chopped pecans

1 small can mandarin orange slices, drained

1 tsp salt • ¼ tsp pepper

¼ tsp thyme • ¼ tsp nutmeg

¼ tsp cinnamon • 6 ounces cream cheese

2 cans refrigerated crescent roll dough

An hour before preparing recipe, soak cranberries in 1/4 cup warm water. In a large saucepan, melt butter. Add celery and apple and sauté lightly. Add chicken, drained cranberries, pecans, and oranges. In a large bowl, combine salt, pepper, thyme, nutmeg, and cinnamon. Combine spice mixture with cream cheese. Add chicken mixture to cream cheese. Gently combine until well mixed. Unroll crescent triangles. Using your fingers, pinch two together forming a square and set on a lightly greased cookie sheet. Place 2 tblsps of chicken mixture in the middle of each square. Fold dough over the top. Bake at 350 degrees until lightly browned.

SPICED PEACH MUFFINS

4½ cups King Arthur unbleached all-purpose flour

1 tsp salt • 4 ½ tsps baking powder

2 cups dark brown sugar

½ tsp ground allspice

½ tsp ground nutmeg

1 tsp ground cinnamon

2 eggs • ¾ cup vegetable oil

1 ¼ cups milk

4 peaches, diced and unpeeled, or
3 cups small whole berries or other fruit, diced

granulated sugar

Combine flour, salt, baking powder, brown sugar, allspice, nutmeg, and cinnamon in a large bowl. Stir in eggs, vegetable oil, and milk, then gently stir in fruit. Grease 16 muffin cups and heap batter into cups. (They will be very full.) Sprinkle with granulated sugar. Bake at 400 degrees for 25-30 minutes or until muffins test done.

A PROPER POT OF TEA

Here's how Lillian taught Gloria the steps to brewing tea.

1. *To brew a proper pot of tea, begin with a stovetop kettle and a teapot.*

2. *Fill the kettle with cold tap water and put it on the stove, then fill the teapot with very warm tap water. The warm water "tempers" the pot so that when you pour the boiling water into it, the temperature change won't crack your beautiful china teapot.*

3. *When the water is about to boil, drop one teaspoon of loose tea per person into the pot and add one extra spoonful for the pot.*

4. *Let the water come to a boil, but don't let it boil more than three or four minutes before you pour it over the tea.*

5. *You don't have to let the tea steep for long— three to five minutes should be sufficient. Just don't forget to strain it before you pour it—unless you are using an infuser.*

"It was a rainy day like today," remembered Claudette, "when my Aunt Elizabeth took my sister Suzanne and me on a train to the city for our first visit to a tea room. We felt like such ladies! She bought each of us a locket as a remembrance of our outing. I will never forget the sights and sounds and fragrances of that day!"

One by one, each lady shared a happy memory she had not thought of in a long time. It was lovely to recall such sweet times. And doing so reminded them of a sister to visit, a friend to write, or a mother to thank.

Ruby unrolled her little scroll and read, "'What person has influenced your life the most?' My father bought me my first set of paints and lots of paper. He encouraged me to paint the world around me, and how rich that has made my life!"

"What new thing would you most like to learn?" Suzette looked up wistfully from her scroll. "I wish I could play the piano. I can't sing, so I would like for my fingers to sing for me!"

"I would like to learn how to make tea!" ventured Gloria. At first they all laughed because Gloria was so witty. Then they realized that she was serious. "Not only do I not know how to cook," she admitted, "I don't know how to make a proper pot of tea. And next time, it's my turn to give the tea!"

"Brewing tea is not difficult," encouraged Lillian. "I'll be happy to come over and help you prepare for your tea party."

"Thank you, Lillian." Gloria looked at Lillian with relief and gratitude and then said to the rest of the group, "I'm a little embarrassed to admit it, but I really need help from all of you. My mother thought that much of

Laura slipped out of her chair as Claudette added, "When I can't remember exactly what I should do, I try to do the kindest thing and put other people first. I know that you already do that."

Laura returned to the table with two etiquette books. "I thought I would read what these books say about tea as a refresher for us all." As Laura read from the first book, the women discovered that teatime was not just

etiquette was stuffy and useless, silly rules. She only taught us basic manners to make us civil. But frankly, I often find myself in situations where I feel awkward because I don't know how to do things the right way."

"I know how uncomfortable it can be to not know the right thing to do," sympathized Ruby. "I used an etiquette book to teach myself, and I've found it's such a wonderful tool."

about rigid rules. The etiquette of tea was really quite interesting!

Then Laura opened *Emily Post's Etiquette and a Guide to Modern Manners* by Elizabeth L. Post to her favorite part: "The hostess who, providing no individual tables, expects her guest to balance knife, fork, jam, cream cake, plate, and cup and saucer, all on her knees, should choose her friends in the circus rather than in society."

They all laughed in amusement, but the point was well made. Good teatime manners mirrored the Golden Rule in the Bible—treating others the way we would like to be treated.

"Thank you all so much!" sighed Gloria gratefully. "Now I think I'm ready to host my tea!"

Claudette looked up from her little unfurled scroll. "'What is the best thing that has happened to you today?' I don't even have to think about that! It's being here with my friends!" She looked toward her kind hostess. "Laura, you really haven't shared much about yourself. What is the nicest thing that has happened to you today?"

Laura couldn't keep from smiling as she announced, "I found out today that I'm going to have a baby! My husband and I have waited ten years for a baby."

Everyone rejoiced with Laura over such blessed news. Almost immediately they all

TEATIME ETIQUETTE FROM LAURA'S BOOK

Here's what Laura read to her guests…

"A tray with teapot, sugar and creamers, and a bowl of lemon slices is brought to one end of the table. Teacups, spoons, and napkins may be carried in on the tea tray or placed on the table. At a large, formal tea, coffee service is placed on a tray at the opposite end of the table. Sugar cubes may be served in a bowl with tongs or sugar may be granular and served with a spoon. The hostess may ask one or two friends to do the honor of pouring the tea so that she can give attention to all her guests at a large tea. Tea bags are discouraged because they are so messy! The tea is poured and handed to each guest one at a time so it will stay hot. The food is self-service, with the guests helping themselves. It is proper to return for seconds after everyone has been served. Tea may be served buffet style on a dining table with individual tables set up for eating, or guests may sit around the dining table."

began to think of having a baby shower tea for her.

"We will pray for this baby's safe arrival," volunteered Claudette, "and help you to prepare." They all nodded in agreement as Laura wiped away tears of joy.

"Laura," began Suzette, "you have made this such a wonderful afternoon for us all! I have so many sweet memories of special times and special places that I had almost forgotten. How lovely it is to look back and share our pasts, and how exciting it is to look forward to new experiences in the future!"

"I like to record my experiences and my memories in a journal," confided Laura, "so I won't forget all the good things that have happened to me. I also use a journal to give a voice to all my hopes and dreams.

"To encourage all of you to share my joy of journaling, I've prepared these journals as gifts. Throughout the pages, I have written questions to encourage you all to do good deeds and to guide you as you record the gifts of your days—people and experiences too precious to forget."

The ladies picked up their new journals and flipped through the pages, glancing at Laura's questions. They couldn't wait to

LAURA'S QUESTIONS

Here are some of the questions Laura recorded in the journals…

- *If I could spend a whole afternoon with a pot of tea and nothing to do but think, what would I think about?*

- *What person meant the most to me today?*

- *If I could do something nice for that person, what would I do?*

- *How did my faith help me today?*

- *How did my faith help someone else today?*

- *What was my best opportunity to show someone love today?*

- *What did I want to be when I grew up? Is what I became even better?*

- *What are my ten best blessings today?*

find a cozy corner at home and start writing in these delightful books. Surely the first entry in everyone's journal would be the same—a description of the delightful party Laura had given them.

Sandy Lynam Clough

Gloria's Tea

AS CLAUDETTE SIPPED HER MORNING tea, she watched through her kitchen window as a wren couple flew back and forth tirelessly building a nest. She was impressed with their choice of real estate! They had chosen to build their nest inside the watering can she had left perched on the rail of her back porch.

The little birds flew down through the top opening of the watering can over and over again, but the nest was so deep inside that Claudette could not see it. Not only would the partial covering on the top of the watering can shelter the nest from  blowing rain, the cat would never think of looking in it! The wrens had done well in finding a safe place to shelter and nurture their young. Claudette was so glad she had not grabbed the can and thoughtlessly filled it with water.

As she watched the wrens a little longer, Claudette thought about Gloria's tea today. She felt that, much like the birds, she had finally found a safe place for fledgling young friendships to grow. The tea society was a place where hurts could be shared, confidences kept, and joys multiplied.

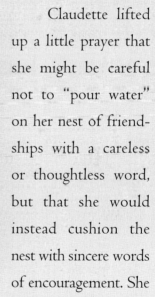

Claudette lifted up a little prayer that she might be careful not to "pour water" on her nest of friendships with a careless or thoughtless word, but that she would instead cushion the nest with sincere words of encouragement. She said a quick "amen," remembering that she still needed to pack her favorite teacup in her basket for the trip to the park.

Claudette breathed in the fresh air as she set out for the party. It was such a glorious spring day that Gloria's idea for an

Gloria's
TEA MENU

Chicken Salad Croissant Sandwiches

Pound Cake with Lemon Curd

Strawberries with Whipped Cream

Brownies

Raspberry Tea

The beauty of Gloria's tea is that there is no cooking involved. Each item can be purchased at a grocery store, deli, or bakery, ready-made.

In her invitation, Gloria had asked each lady to wear her hat from Claudette's party and a white dress, and to bring a teacup and saucer, dessert plate, and silver and napkins in a basket. At the park, they would randomly swap baskets for the afternoon and enjoy each other's favorite teacups!

Claudette, Laura, Ruby, and Suzette had agreed to assemble in front of the church so they could walk to the park together and meet Gloria and Lillian there. As they set out, skirts brushing the pansies along the edge of the sidewalk and eyes gazing at dogwood blossoms drifting overhead, they were a vision of springtime loveliness in their white dresses. When they arrived at a stream that gently cascaded over moss-covered rocks on the far side of the park, the ladies saw that Gloria had chosen a large rock beside the stream for a table and covered it with a white Battenberg lace tablecloth. She had also thoughtfully

outdoor tea in the park seemed almost inspired. True to her word, Lillian had gone to Gloria's house ahead of time to help her make tea. Gloria could then take it to the park in a jug and transfer it to a teapot there. Lillian had even accompanied Gloria to the market, where Gloria had made excellent choices for teatime treats.

provided soft afghans to cover the rocks that were to serve as seats. The afghans would keep their white dresses clean. A quilt was spread out on the ground.

Gloria collected the various baskets from the ladies, then randomly passed them out to their new owners for the afternoon. Next she transferred raspberry tea from her jug to a silver teapot. As Lillian poured the tea, Gloria sliced pound cake and spread the slices with lemon curd. Already on her rock "table" was a plate of luscious, ripe strawberries with whipped cream for dipping and brownies from the bakery. Sliced croissants filled with chicken salad sat on another plate. Gloria was amazed and surprised at herself. She really could give a tea!

As the ladies lifted the teacups out of the baskets, each found a surprise from the owner

of the cup placed inside. They had all added something that the recipient could keep after the cup and utensils were returned: a card, a poem, a packet of flower seeds, a blessing, a few chocolates. As the ladies arrived, Gloria had slipped a gift into each basket. She had pressed tiny ferns and violets weeks earlier and framed them in little gold frames.

The tea society had thought of getting Gloria a cookbook as a hostess gift, but then decided she might be happier right now not knowing how to cook. Instead they presented her with a compass, in the hopes that not only would she always find her way home from her nature walks, but that all the directions of her life would be good ones!

As soon as they finished their tea, off came Gloria's and Claudette's shoes. They lifted up their long skirts and squealed with

delight as they sat on the rocks and dangled their feet into the creek, wiggling their toes in the cold water.

As Suzette wandered off to pick wildflowers on the edge of the woods, Ruby said, "Please wait! I brought my sketchbook to record our afternoon. Suzette, come sit on this rock in the middle of the stream. I want to paint you holding your teacup, contemplating the beauty of the day."

Suzette carefully made her way across the stream on the slippery rocks, but as she stepped up to the rock that was to be her chair, she slipped. Her foot gave way on the moss below as her dress tore and her knee scraped across the rock. Breaking her fall with her hands, she dropped the teacup and saucer—Claudette's teacup and saucer!

As her treasures shattered on the rock,

tears welled up in Claudette's eyes. She quickly blinked them back as she remembered how her mother had taught her that things were meant to be used and friendships were meant to be treasured. It was important now that she follow her mother's advice to hold things loosely and to hold friends dearly.

Claudette turned her attention to comforting her friend before Suzette began to cry. Moving quickly to smooth an awkward moment, she made little of her own loss, letting no one know the cup had been her mother's. As Gloria shook the water out of Suzette's shoes, Lillian wrapped one of the afghans around her and promised to mend her dress and make it as good as new.

Apologizing profusely, Suzette offered to replace Claudette's cup with her own.

THE SKY'S THE LIMIT

Gloria chose a park for her tea party,
but there are plenty of outdoor options.
Be creative in your choices and your friends
will be sure to remember their first al fresco
tea party. Here are some suggestions:

Backyard • Arboretum • Balcony
Rooftop • Gazebo • Rose Garden • Deck
Beach • Boat • Lake • Nature Center
Concert in the Park • Front Porch

Almost simultaneously, Laura, Ruby, Lillian, and Gloria offered their own teacups to Claudette as well!

There were no more tears in Claudette's eyes to blink back. Her mother had left Claudette her own teacups to encourage her to stay connected to kindred hearts and to nurture good friendships. And here they were! With this group, she no longer needed a teacup to remind her of that.

As soon as the pieces of broken teacup were picked up, Claudette took the opportunity to turn the focus of the group to what was really important in their lives. Even though Suzette wanted to apologize one more time, Claudette assured her that no apology was needed.

"We love these teacups," Claudette said, "but for all of their delicate beauty, they are only tools—beautiful tools that we can use to craft a friendship or to create time with a friend. The lovely dresses we like to wear, our stylish hats, the fashionable shoes we use for special occasions—all of these are just tools for building friendships. Styles will come and styles will go, but it's the friendships which last that I'm so grateful for."

Ruby had brought her sketchbook to Gloria's tea to make drawings for a painting of Sandy's Tea Society. But it was Claudette who had painted a beautiful picture of their friendship.

Sandy Lynam Clough

Ruby's Tea

LAURA HAD SPREAD THE WORD TO everyone except Ruby. So Ruby was surprised and overwhelmed when the rest of the tea society appeared on her doorstep with five frozen meals! After Ruby had planned her tea, she had received commissions for three paintings. Five prepared meals surely would help her to meet her deadlines. Here she had been spending time making a special afternoon for her friends, and now they were more than giving her time back to her!

As Ruby welcomed the ladies of the tea society into her home, expressing her gratitude for the meals, it was all she could do to keep from staring at their feet. But she quickly excused herself to store the food.

While Ruby was gone, the ladies exclaimed over their hostess' decor. The way Ruby had used teacups to decorate everything from her chandelier to her chairs and windows was so charming that nobody even noticed she had forgotten to buy flowers for a centerpiece. (The truth is, Ruby never remembers to buy flowers unless she plans to paint them!)

In spite of having so much to look at, when Ruby returned from the kitchen, she noticed that all of her friends' eyes were downcast. Oh, they weren't discouraged—they were curious, for Ruby had invited them to a shoe tea! The invitation she had sent out asked each lady to create a unique pair of shoes and then wear them to the tea. Ruby had also noted that the shoes should share a message.

Now as the ladies looked down from one to another, they had one question on their minds: What were their feet saying?

Rather than having her guests peer under the table at teatime, Ruby turned off the boiling water and invited the ladies to put their chairs in a circle, sit down, and have their fashion show. Tea could wait. Right now, shoes were far more interesting!

Ruby asked Laura to show her shoes first. As Laura stood up and walked to the center of the circle, she lifted her skirt ankle-high to reveal shoes that matched her black and ivory dress. In black script, Laura had  written encouraging words on her ivory shoes. In her beautiful handwriting were the words: *faith, hope, love, joy, kindness, patience, loyalty,* and *goodness.* "I decorated my shoes like this," she said, "because I always want to be careful to share encouragement as I go along my way."

Suzette was next. She had glued potpourri all over her shoes so that they were covered with fragments of flowers, and on top of each shoe she had fastened a big silk rose. "I want to try to leave the fragrance of a sweet spirit everywhere I go," she explained.

When her turn came, Claudette modeled shoes that would remind her how wonderful it was to be feminine, even when she was doing chores. She had completely covered her shoes with pearls and old jewelry. "I can certainly feel like a queen in these shoes, even when I'm washing dishes," she said.

Ruby stood up next and lifted one side of her skirt to reveal a plain black pump. Surely she had just run out of time—it wasn't at all like Ruby to miss a chance to be creative! Then she revealed her other foot. Perched on top of that black pump was a little white mouse! The ladies all squealed as they thought it might run up her leg, and then the "eeks!" gave way to peals of laughter as they realized the mouse wasn't real. As one by one they regained their composure and wiped tears of laughter from their eyes, Ruby explained with the straightest face she could muster, "I want to remember to help someone laugh every day."

Gloria insisted that everyone close her eyes before she stood up. When she was sure nobody could see, she began to walk across the room. As bells tinkled, Lillian asked, "Are they Christmas bells?"

"School bells?" wondered Suzette.

"Is there a cat?" asked Ruby as she raised her feet in mock fear.

"No," said Gloria, "they're wedding bells!" As the ladies opened their eyes, they saw that Gloria was wearing exquisite white satin shoes covered with lace. Cascading down the heel of each shoe were two silver bells and lily-of-the-valley blossoms.

"My beau has proposed!" exclaimed Gloria.

How happy was the tea society for their newly engaged friend! Their excited questions sounded like popcorn popping. "When is the wedding date?" "Where did he ask you?" "Show us the ring!" "When did he ask you?" "What were you wearing?" "Does your father like him?"

For a moment it seemed as if Gloria had five mothers as well as five best friends!

Ruby finally pointed out that Lillian had yet to model her shoes. As they all sat down again, Lillian

RUBY'S TEA TABLE

Ruby used teacups as the decorating theme for her tea table.
She had so many creative ideas!

- *Using wire ribbon, she tied teacups by their handles*
to the chandelier over her table.

- *She wrapped the backs of her chairs with ribbon and tied a teacup*
in the center of each chair back with a bow, weaving ivy through it.
She also wove ivy through the chandelier.

- *She gathered up her window swags and accented them with*
a teacup on each side. She twined more ivy around the swags.

- *Around the edge of the table, she created a swag garland with two*
strands of beads. Every twelve inches, she brought the strands up to
the edge of the table and pinned them from underneath. She also attached
a pretty demitasse spoon with a bow on it from underneath. The pearls
seemed to be caught up by the spoons as they gracefully circled the table!

stood up and slowly raised her skirt to her ankles. Her black silk pumps were edged in rhinestones, and the heel was bejeweled with flowers of rhinestones. "I made these shoes," she said with a twinkle in her eye, "for waltzing in the moonlight."

That did it! Everyone in the tea society wanted a pair of shoes like Lillian's.

included a teapot, a sugar and creamer set, some plates, and enough teacups and saucers for seven. The assortment of patterns was rich and colorful, making the china alone a feast for the eyes. A large black embroidered and fringed piano shawl covered the table, reaching to the floor. It was topped by a smaller plain white tablecloth.

Now that the suspense of the shoes was over, the ladies were eager to get back to the lovely table setting awaited them. Ruby quickly began to prepare orange and black pekoe tea as her guests moved toward the dining room. She had set the table with her collection of chintzware china, which

The ladies were delighted to see that Ruby had cut cucumber sandwiches into the shapes of shoes with a shoe-shaped cookie cutter. She had prepared Sandy's Tea Society Cream to spread on chocolate chip and orange scones. A plum tart displayed next to a plate of green and purple grapes added

THE CHARM OF CHINTZ

Chintzware china is a charming floral tableware that is highly collectible. The richly hued patterns of flowers and ornate birds of the fabric "chintz" became more accessible when transfer printing on earthenware was made available in the late 1880s. Originally made in England, the china was produced as everyday ware even though each intricate pattern had to be transferred by hand from a lithograph to the actual piece. Chintzware comes in all shapes and sizes from teapots and teacups to complete dinnerware sets and vases. The most highly sought after pieces are those that were produced by the English companies Royal Winton, Lord Nelson Ware, James Kent Ltd., and Crown Ducal.

an extra touch of color. Then they saw the mice! Ruby had made a tray of little white chocolate mice!

Ruby had found six little ceramic or glass shoes in antique stores. These she had filled with strawberry silk, which she now

Sandy Lynam Clough

served to each lady with a brand-new shoehorn as the spoon. As they savored the delicious fare Ruby had prepared for them, they talked about shoes. Ruby tried to name all the colors of shoes she had ever owned:

"Pink, red, silver, pumpkin, yellow, purple, green, and, of course, ruby!"

Claudette was embarrassed to say that once she had dressed in such a hurry that she had arrived at a party with her bedroom slippers on.

Lillian admitted that, at her first ball, she had added a bit too much flourish to her waltz and had kicked her shoe off.

After dressing in the early hours, Suzette had once looked down at her feet to find that her shoes did not match.

Laura confessed to having persistent dreams about going out only to find herself barefoot. That would be the worst, they all agreed—to be without shoes!

After the ladies finished their strawberry silk, Ruby quickly washed the glass and ceramic shoes and presented them to their guests as keepsakes of the day. And what a day it was! As the ladies said their good-byes and talked about their next tea, they took one last look at each other's shoes. How delightful it was to learn about each other!

Ruby's
TEA MENU

Cucumber Sandwiches

Chocolate Chip and Orange Scones
with Sandy's Tea Society Cream

Plum Tart

Assorted Grapes

Little White Chocolate Mice

Strawberry Silk

Orange and Black Pekoe Tea

CUCUMBER SANDWICHES

1 package Ranch salad dressing mix
12 ounces soft cream cheese
1/2 cup mayonnaise (or enough to make spreading consistent)
1 cucumber • 1 loaf of your favorite bread
seasoned salt • dill

Mix first three ingredients together. Let sit overnight or for several hours in refrigerator. Using any shape cookie cutter, cut shapes from bread. (Ruby used a shoe-shaped cookie cutter.) Cut cucumber into thin slices. Spread bread with sandwich spread. Add cucumber slices and sprinkle with seasoned salt. Top with matching bread shape and garnish with fresh dill.

LITTLE WHITE CHOCOLATE MICE

1 package chocolate-covered graham crackers • 1 bag Hershey's white chocolate Hugs
2 bags semi-sweet chocolate chips • 1 jar red maraschino cherries (with stems)
1 small bag sliced almonds • 1 tube black gel icing

NOTE: THIS WORKS BEST IF YOU MAKE IT WITH A PARTNER WHO CAN HELP YOU WITH THE DIFFERENT STEPS. Lay out graham crackers on a large cookie sheet. Space them about 1"-1½" apart so you can easily work with them. Open up the jar of cherries and drain before using. Place Hershey's Hugs in a bowl nearby. In a saucepan, melt one bag of semi-sweet chocolate chips on low heat. After chips have melted, roll cherries in chocolate and place them on the graham crackers. (Place the cherries in the center with the stems pointing up as "tails.") Right after you place the cherry on the graham cracker, place a Hershey's Hug on the front to form the mouse face. Then add two slices of almond for the ears. Only make as many chocolate-covered cherries as you can before the chocolate dries. As you need them, you can melt more chocolate chips. When finished, place two small eyes and a nose on the Hershey Hug face with black gel icing.

PLUM TART

1 tart crust, your favorite recipe
1¼ pounds fresh (or canned and drained) plums
⅔ cup sugar • 2 tblsps lemon juice
¼ tsp lemon zest • 1½ tblsps cornstarch

Mix sugar, cornstarch, lemon juice, and lemon zest together in a large bowl. Add pitted, sliced plums and stir. Spread on tart crust and bake at 375 degrees for 30 minutes. Serve at room temperature.

STRAWBERRY SILK

1½ pints fresh hulled strawberries • ½ cup sugar
2 drops lemon juice • 1 cup whipping cream

Puree strawberries, sugar, and lemon juice in food processor fitted with steel blade. Whip cream until it holds stiff peaks, then stir the puree in until mixture is smooth. Adjust for sweetness, if desired. Refrigerate for several hours before serving.

CHOCOLATE CHIP ORANGE SCONES

2 cups all-purpose flour • ½ cup sugar
½ tsp baking powder • ½ tsp salt
½ cup butter, chilled • 2 eggs
¼ cup frozen orange juice concentrate
1 tsp vanilla • 1 cup mini semisweet chocolate chips

In a large bowl, mix together flour, sugar, baking powder, and salt. Cut the butter into small pieces on top of flour mixture. Using a pastry blender or two knives, cut the butter into the flour mixture until it resembles coarse crumbs. In a separate bowl, stir together eggs, orange juice, and vanilla. Combine with the flour mixture. Dough will be very moist. With floured hands, knead in the chocolate chips until mixed well. Do not over-handle the dough. Turn dough out onto a lightly floured cookie sheet and shape into an 8- or 9-inch circle. With a serrated knife, cut into 8 wedges. Bake for 20 to 25 minutes at 425 degrees. Remove from oven and cool on a wire rack for 10 minutes. Serve warm.

Lillian's Tea

LILLIAN BREATHED IN THE FRAGRANCE of an antique rose as she pruned the rose bushes surrounding her terrace. "What could be more romantic than roses?" she absentmindedly asked herself. The answer suddenly came to her: "Roses in the moonlight! My tea will be a romantic moonlight tea." And the only way to make it a truly romantic tea was to make it formal and invite men. For the first time, the tea society would include husbands and boyfriends as guests. By the time Lillian had gotten into the house with the pruning shears and a basket of roses, she had her whole tea party planned. Inside would be candlelight, outside would be moonlight.

Friends could never decide whether there were more roses inside Lillian's house or outside in the garden. The evening of her tea party, it was a tie. Ruby had offered to come early to help with last-minute details while Lillian went upstairs to slip into her evening gown. Everything seemed to be under control, so Ruby took time to admire the beautiful rooms. The walls were papered with a beautiful rose pattern. China plates, cups, saucers, and platters were displayed in an open cupboard—every one with a different rose pattern.

Lillian had made a floor-length pink dotted Swiss tablecloth for the party. It was topped by a tulle tablecloth on which she had

GIFTS FROM THE GARDEN

Antique roses—prized for their beautiful blooms, luxurious fragrance, and low maintenance—have long been a favorite among rose enthusiasts all over the world. Varieties that were cultivated before 1867 are the rootstock from which present-day roses garner their heritage and are generally classified as antique. In 1803, Empress Josephine of France championed their cause by mandating the botanists of her day develop more than 250 varieties to fill her spectacular gardens at Malmaison. From palacial gardens to country cottage backyards, they have flourished ever since. Below are a few beloved antique varieties:

EMPRESS JOSEPHINE (1853)

Named inhonor of the empress who encouraged its development. This royal rose produces large, fragrant double pink blooms that are delicately edged in darker pink.

CARDINAL DE RICHELIEU (1840)

Probably one of the oldest and most famous of the antique Gallica roses. Its succulent dark purple blooms put ona spectacular display in summer.

CELSIANA (1750)

This Damascena rose captures a gardener's heart with is delicate pink blooms and rich, golden stamens that are dramatically framed with lush, gray-green foliage.

randomly pinned silk roses. They almost seemed to float!

The chairbacks were wrapped in tulle, which Lillian had gathered and pinned with silk roses. She had covered the chair cushions in pink dotted Swiss and had made ruffles for her napkins out of the same material.

In the living room, the rose-colored moiré swags were fastened by rosettes Lillian had made from the same fabric. Over the dining room windows, garlands of silk roses and ivy intertwined with white twinkle lights.

Three small tables—these also covered in pink dotted Swiss—had been moved to the living room. Each was large enough to seat two couples. By each place sat a little cream pitcher. Inside the pitcher, a votive candle floated in water. In the center of each table was, of course, a bouquet of roses.

Lillian told Ruby that she had appointed "conversation captains" for each table. As she did want the men to become friends, she'd ruled out politics as a discussion topic. And the ladies (with the exception of Gloria, of course) might be left out if the men only talked about sports all evening. Therefore, Lillian had decided that the ladies would engage the gentlemen in pleasant conversation by asking them about their most interesting travels.

Lillian descended the stairs just as the doorbell rang. As she welcomed each couple, she presented them with a rose corsage and boutonnière to pin on each other. How handsome and elegant everyone looked! Laura presented Lillian with a box of beautiful rose-scented candles as a "thank you" from the whole group.

Ruby suppressed a giggle as she noticed the ladies' shoes as they stepped through the

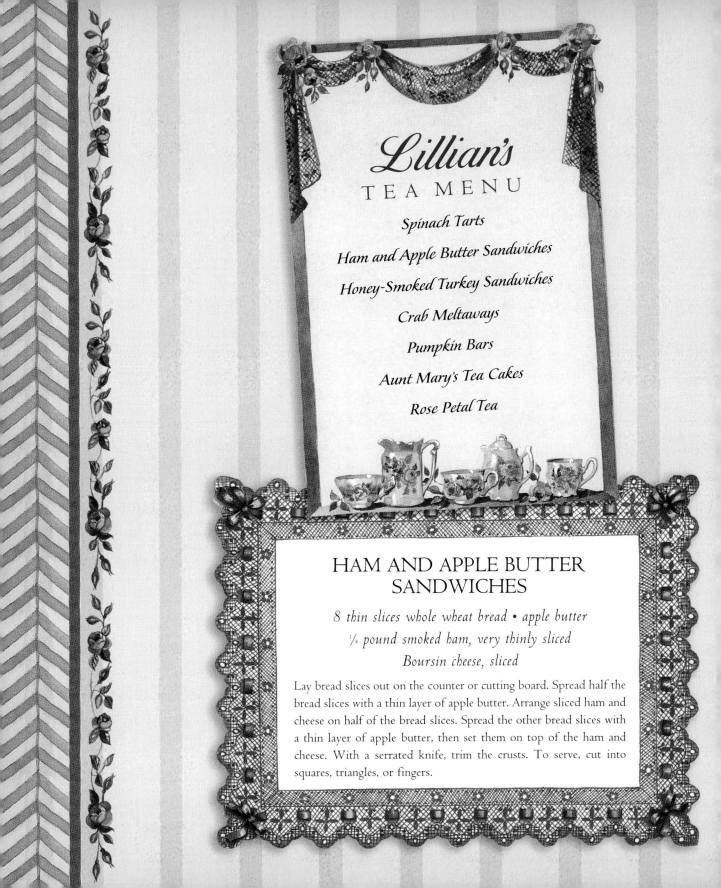

Lillian's
TEA MENU

Spinach Tarts

Ham and Apple Butter Sandwiches

Honey-Smoked Turkey Sandwiches

Crab Meltaways

Pumpkin Bars

Aunt Mary's Tea Cakes

Rose Petal Tea

HAM AND APPLE BUTTER SANDWICHES

8 thin slices whole wheat bread • apple butter
¼ pound smoked ham, very thinly sliced
Boursin cheese, sliced

Lay bread slices out on the counter or cutting board. Spread half the bread slices with a thin layer of apple butter. Arrange sliced ham and cheese on half of the bread slices. Spread the other bread slices with a thin layer of apple butter, then set them on top of the ham and cheese. With a serrated knife, trim the crusts. To serve, cut into squares, triangles, or fingers.

SPINACH TART

10 premade pastry cups

2 packages frozen spinach

1 red onion, chopped • 2 cloves garlic, chopped

4 stalks celery, minced • ½ cup parsley, chopped

¼ cup chives, chopped

3 tblsps fresh savory, chopped

1 tblsp lemon juice

1 cup olive oil • 6 eggs, beaten

2 ½ cups sharp cheddar cheese, grated

½ cup bread crumbs • ½ cup olive oil

salt • pepper

Preheat oven to 250 degrees. Grease 2 large cookie sheets. Thaw spinach. Place spinach with its juice, celery, onion, and garlic in the bowl of a food processor; blend briefly. Add olive oil, parsley, and herbs; blend again. Add eggs, cheese, and salt and pepper to taste; blend for 3 seconds. Pour mixture into pastry cups. Sprinkle the top with bread crumbs, then dribble with a little olive oil. Bake 4 to 4½ hours; tart will be dry and slightly crisp.

HONEY-SMOKED TURKEY SANDWICHES

½ cup unsalted butter, softened

2 tsp orange juice concentrate

1 tsp fresh ginger root, grated

1 loaf white bread, thinly sliced

½ pound honey-smoked turkey, sliced

Add ginger to juice. In a bowl, whisk together butter and juice. Spread a thin layer of orange butter on a slice of bread and place a slice of smoked turkey on top. Cut out heart shapes from bread using cookie cutter.

CRAB MELTAWAYS

1 8-ounce can crab meat, drained

1 jar Kraft Old English Cheddar Cheese

½ tsp garlic salt • 1 dozen mini bagels

Mix together first three ingredients in a small bowl. Cut bagels in half and spread with cheese mixture. Place on a cookie sheet and bake for 15 minutes at 350 degrees.

Note: These can be prepared ahead of time and frozen before baking. Add 5 minutes to the baking time if baked frozen.

PUMPKIN BARS

2 cups all purpose flour

2 tsp cinnamon • 1 tblsp baking powder

2 cups canned pumpkin (without spices)

½ tsp salt • 2 tsp baking soda

2 cups sugar • 4 eggs

1 cup vegetable oil

Mix all ingredients together by hand in a large mixing bowl. Pour into a greased 9x13 baking pan. Bake at 350 degrees for 30 minutes. Cool and frost.

CREAM CHEESE FROSTING

1 box powdered sugar

8 ounces cream cheese, softened

½ stick butter, softened • 1 tsp vanilla

½ cup chopped walnuts • milk

Mix all the ingredients in a bowl. Add small amounts of milk (if necessary) to get the desired consistency. Spread on pumpkin bars.

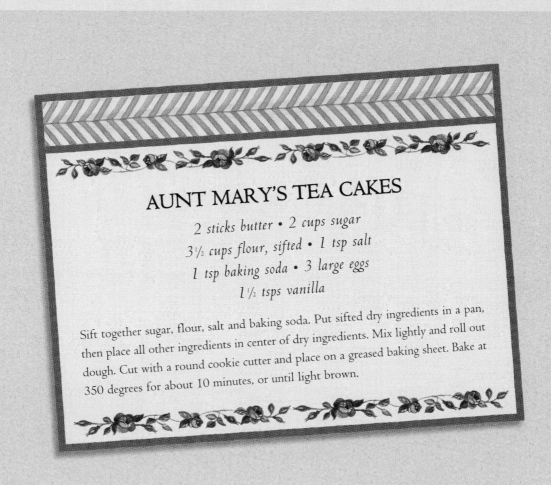

AUNT MARY'S TEA CAKES

2 sticks butter • 2 cups sugar
3½ cups flour, sifted • 1 tsp salt
1 tsp baking soda • 3 large eggs
1½ tsps vanilla

Sift together sugar, flour, salt and baking soda. Put sifted dry ingredients in a pan, then place all other ingredients in center of dry ingredients. Mix lightly and roll out dough. Cut with a round cookie cutter and place on a greased baking sheet. Bake at 350 degrees for about 10 minutes, or until light brown.

door. They all had on black fabric pumps with rhinestones around the edge of the sole, a beautiful brooch on the toe, and rhinestones cascading down the back of the heel. "It's going to be a very romantic evening!" she remarked to herself. She whirled around to go and help Lillian fill the teapots, revealing shoes completely covered in rhinestones.

As Ruby poured the rose petal tea, Lillian made certain that every guest was seated comfortably at a table and served plenty of delicious food. Her menu, which included savory as well as sweet foods, was hearty enough to actually be a dinner.

Along with spinach tarts were ham and apple butter sandwiches, honey-smoked

LILLIAN'S ROMANTIC MUSIC

Lillian had selected several special pieces for the musicians to play during her romantic moonlight tea:

WALTZ IN A MINOR
by Frederic Chopin

VALSE SENTIMENTALE
by Franz Schubert

TWO MELODIES, OPUS 3, NO. 1:
MELODY IN F MAJOR
by Anton Rubenstein

RHAPSODY ON A THEME OF
PAGANINI, OPUS 43 VARIATION NO. 18
by Sergei Rachmaninov

SYMPHONIE FANTASTIQUE:
SECOND MOVEMENT (UN BAL)
by Hectoe Berlioz

INVITATION TO THE DANCE
by Carl Maria von Weber

THREE ROMANTIC WALTZES
by Emmanuel Chabrier

turkey sandwiches (cut in the shape of hearts), crab meltaways, pumpkin bars, and her Aunt Mary's teacakes. Lillian hoped to use good food and pleasant company to engage the gentlemen in an enthusiasm for taking tea.

After the meal, as Lillian cleared away the plates and teacups, Laura noticed a melody coming from the garden. "Listen," she said in a hushed voice.

They could all hear it now. Lillian opened the French doors to her garden, wide and beautiful music filled the room from a harp and violin. She had hired two music students to play waltzes for them on the terrace. Twinkling lights were twined through her rose bushes, but the main glow came from the moonlight. Finally, it dawned on the gentlemen what the ladies in the society had known all along. The tea was an excuse for waltzing in the moonlight!

Sandy Lynam Clough

Suzette's Tea

SINCE SHE HAD ON AN OLD housedress, Suzette decided it was as good a time as any to test one of her dining room chairs. She sat down, leaned back, and stood up again. Good! She wasn't stuck to the chair. It had passed the first test. Walking over to her hall mirror, Suzette stretched and strained to look over her shoulder at the back of her dress. Good again! She didn't have a blue seat. The chairs were dry and ready for her tea party that afternoon.

Suzette was confident that it didn't matter to her friends if she didn't have fancy dining room furniture, and it certainly wasn't an issue for her. But she had wanted to brighten things up for her party, so she'd painted her dining room chairs a fresh shade of blue. The chairs were now the perfect

accent to the floor-length yellow gingham tablecloth that adorned her round table. A large square of cotton eyelet fabric edged with an eyelet ruffle made a proper tea covering for the table.

Suzette's kitchen sink was filled with fresh flowers from her cottage garden. She had gathered the blooms that morning before the dew could dry. From that stash, she pulled daisies, lilies, bachelor buttons, irises, and roses to fill a watering can that sat on her table. Fresh ivy spilled out of the can and trailed onto the table.

On a tray she arranged her teapot, sugar bowl, and creamer—all blue and white china (though none of it matched). In fact, every room of Suzette's house was decorated with

SUZETTE'S FLOWER CORSAGES

LAURA
Yellow rose — Friendship

RUBY
Deep red rose — Love & joy

CLAUDETTE
Ivory hydrangea — Devoted

GLORIA
Shell-pink rose — Femininity

LILLIAN
Rose-colored rose — Grace & beauty

SUZETTE
Daisy — Cheerfulness

Suzette observed that each of her friends had a "signature" flower. With a little research, she found the virtue that matched each flower—and also complimented her friend! Relieved that no one identified with exotic blossoms that were hard to find, Suzette matched everyone with her favorite flower.

To make the corsages, Suzette taped the stems of the flowers together with florist's tape and then rested the blossoms upright in water. Just before her guests arrived, she added a pretty white ribbon tied in a bow to each corsage. On the sashes, she used gold ink to write the friend's name and the special meaning of the flower. She tucked in some little fern fronds as a final touch.

pieces of blue and white china in many different patterns. The classic color combination was attractive with everything.

Even though Suzette had a red living room and a yellow dining room, the blue and white combination was a perfect accent in both rooms, especially along with colorful bouquets of garden flowers. And flowers were certainly the theme of this tea party!

By carefully watching how each of her friends in the tea society dressed and decorated, Suzette had discovered that each lady had a favorite flower. From  her garden she had picked these special blooms and made corsages for her guests.

Suzette began to arrange the splendid assortment of party foods she had prepared, setting them on blue and white china plates and platters. After she had placed zucchini lemon muffins, springtime tea sandwiches, apricot jam tea sandwiches, and a peach torte on the table, she wound fresh ivy around the plates and platters. She placed her favorite scones—white chocolate and ginger apricot—in a little basket lined with white paper doilies. And, of course, a dish of Sandy's Tea Society Cream also sat on the table.

Right at three o'clock Suzette heard a chorus of voices outside her door. Quickly, she poured her summer garden tea into the teapot. Then she rushed to the door with her basket of corsages to pin one on each guest's dress as she welcomed her. The ladies found that Suzette's home lived up to the word on their hostess' corsage—cheerful. The thoughtfulness of the corsages reminded them that there was indeed a fragrance of Suzette's sweet spirit everywhere she was.

On the table was another surprise for the ladies. Suzette had scouted tag sales and antique stores in a quest for a teacup and saucer for each of her friends that was adorned with her "signature" flower. She had pulled a pretty printed vintage hankie in coordinating colors through the handle of

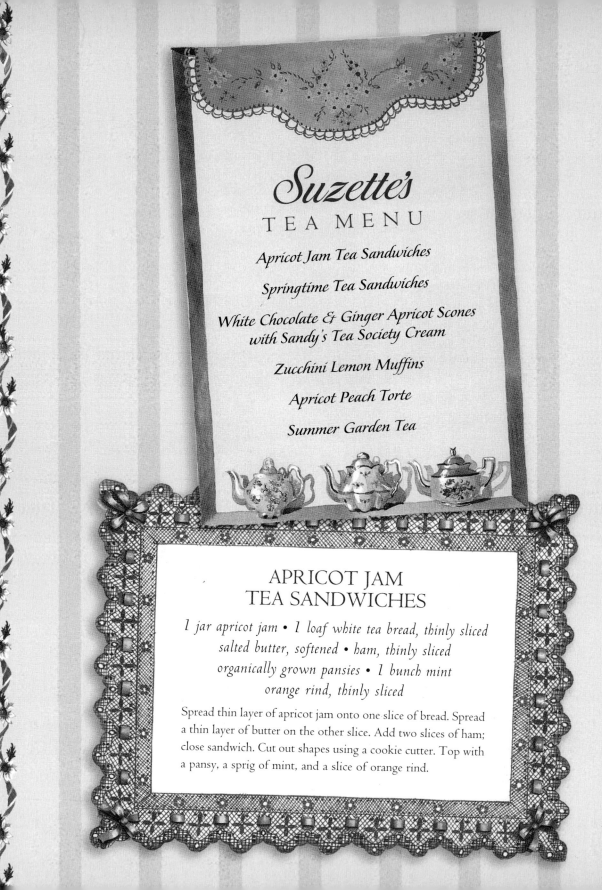

Suzette's
TEA MENU

Apricot Jam Tea Sandwiches

Springtime Tea Sandwiches

*White Chocolate & Ginger Apricot Scones
with Sandy's Tea Society Cream*

Zucchini Lemon Muffins

Apricot Peach Torte

Summer Garden Tea

APRICOT JAM
TEA SANDWICHES

*1 jar apricot jam • 1 loaf white tea bread, thinly sliced
salted butter, softened • ham, thinly sliced
organically grown pansies • 1 bunch mint
orange rind, thinly sliced*

Spread thin layer of apricot jam onto one slice of bread. Spread
a thin layer of butter on the other slice. Add two slices of ham;
close sandwich. Cut out shapes using a cookie cutter. Top with
a pansy, a sprig of mint, and a slice of orange rind.

SUMMER GARDEN TEA

2 tblsps granulated sugar
3 whole cloves • 1 cinnamon stick
2 tea bags • 2 cups apricot nectar
⅓ cup undiluted frozen orange juice concentrate
1 quart water • 8 ounces white grape juice
8 fresh orange slices
8 fresh strawberries, washed with stems intact

In a small saucepan, combine the first five ingredients, stirring well. Simmer for 5 minutes, then steep for 15 minutes. Strain the tea into a glass container and add the apricot nectar and orange juice concentrate. Mix together and let cool. Pour the tea over ice in a glass, then add water to each glass. Add one ounce of grape juice and a splash of orange juice concentrate to each glass. Garnish each glass with an orange slice and a strawberry. Serve chilled.

ZUCCHINI LEMON MUFFINS

2 cups King Arthur unbleached all-purpose flour
½ cup granulated sugar • 1 tblsp baking powder
1 tsp salt • 1 tbsp lemon peel, grated
½ cup (or more, if desired) chopped walnuts
½ cup (or more, if desired) raisins
2 eggs, beaten • ½ cup milk • ⅓ cup vegetable oil
1 packed cup zucchini, shredded

Preheat oven to 400 degrees. Combine flour, sugar, baking powder, salt, and lemon peel in a large bowl. Stir in walnuts and raisins. In a smaller bowl (or a two-cup liquid measuring cup), combine eggs, milk, and oil. Make a well in the center of the dry ingredients and add the wet ingredients. Stir until just barely combined, then gently fold in zucchini. Spoon the batter into a greased, 12-cup muffin tin. Bake for 20-25 minutes or until muffins spring back when you press them with your fingertips.

SPRINGTIME TEA SANDWICHES

1 small bunch watercress
several radishes, thinly sliced
5 eggs, hard-cooked and shelled
¼ cup mayonnaise
2 tblsps whole-grain Dijon mustard
12 slices firm-textured white bread
12 slices firm-textured wheat bread
¼ cup mayonnaise

Chop eggs and blend with mustard and mayonnaise. Spread white bread slices with egg mixture. Top with wheat bread slices. Spread tops with mayonnaise. Trim off crusts and cut each sandwich into two rectangles. Garnish with watercress leaves and radish slices. May be assembled up to 6 hours before serving. Cover and refrigerate.

APRICOT PEACH TORTE

22 zwieback crackers
1 16-ounce can apricot halves
1 16-ounce can peach halves
1 cup sugar • 3 eggs, beaten
¾ cup sour cream • ½ tsp nutmeg
1½ tsps vanilla • ½ tsp almond extract

In a food processor, turn zwieback crackers into crumbs. Pat 2/3 of crumbs into the bottom of a well-buttered 8" springform pan. Drain peaches and apricots. Place peach halves cut side up on crumbs. Fill in spaces with apricot halves, keeping 3 aside for garnish. Blend together the last 6 ingredients and pour over the fruit. Sprinkle with remaining ⅓ of crumbs and bake at 350 degrees for 1 hour. Cool, then remove from sides of pan. Garnish with apricot halves and dollops of sour cream.

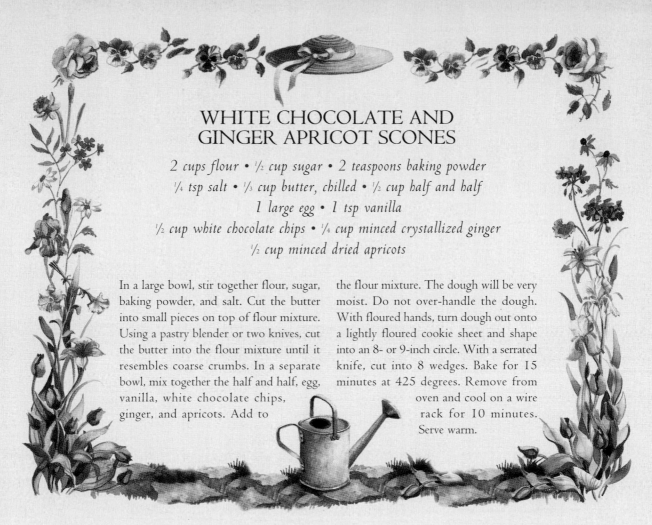

WHITE CHOCOLATE AND GINGER APRICOT SCONES

2 cups flour • ½ cup sugar • 2 teaspoons baking powder
¼ tsp salt • ⅓ cup butter, chilled • ½ cup half and half
1 large egg • 1 tsp vanilla
½ cup white chocolate chips • ¼ cup minced crystallized ginger
½ cup minced dried apricots

In a large bowl, stir together flour, sugar, baking powder, and salt. Cut the butter into small pieces on top of flour mixture. Using a pastry blender or two knives, cut the butter into the flour mixture until it resembles coarse crumbs. In a separate bowl, mix together the half and half, egg, vanilla, white chocolate chips, ginger, and apricots. Add to the flour mixture. The dough will be very moist. Do not over-handle the dough. With floured hands, turn dough out onto a lightly floured cookie sheet and shape into an 8- or 9-inch circle. With a serrated knife, cut into 8 wedges. Bake for 15 minutes at 425 degrees. Remove from oven and cool on a wire rack for 10 minutes. Serve warm.

each teacup. After the tea, these would go home with the ladies as a sincere expression of her friendship.

Suddenly, Gloria remembered that she had forgotten her manners—and the hostess gift! From just inside the door she retrieved the ivy heart-shaped topiary they had brought Suzette. How delighted was Suzette with this gift!

After everyone was seated and served, Ruby asked, "Suzette, when we're done with our tea, may we see the rest of your house? The way you've used rich colors, mixed fabric patterns, and arranged the things you've collected is so appealing. I could learn a lot about decorating from you."

"I'd be happy to take you on a little tour," Suzette smiled. "It's not a grand house,

Sandy Lynam Clough

but a personal house. It's full of things that mean something to me. There is one room that ordinarily I would be embarrassed to show you, but today I'm eager for you to see it because I need help decorating it, and I need help now!"

"Are you expecting company?" asked Claudette.

"Not company—my mother. Her name is Claire, and she's a widow. We've been planning for some time for her to come and live with us. But we didn't expect her house to sell so quickly. I need to turn our spare 'junk' room into a cozy haven for her in just three weeks!"

"What kind of things does your mother like?" Laura wondered.

"Well, she's not very formal, but she loves old handmade things and soft colors. She wouldn't expect or even want everything to be brand new. I guess I want to create a fresh new room for her that, at the same time, is familiar. Do you think that's possible?"

"I think it is," said Lillian.

"This is a project for Sandy's Tea Society!" declared Ruby.

As Suzette led the way to the spare room, her friends followed, looking at what she had to work with and planning as they went.

GLORIA'S IVY HEART-SHAPED TOPIARY

To make the hostess gift that Gloria gave Suzette, take a piece of heavy wire about two feet long. Bend it in half. From that "V" shape, form the two round tops of the heart, then bring the vine down and join the two ends at a point. Twist the ends together and stick them into a pot of soil to anchor the heart. Then plant two sprigs of ivy—one to grow up each side of the heart until they meet at the top.

In the spare room, Suzette opened a trunk full of things that had been passed down to her by her grandmother and some things that had belonged to her mother—all familiar things.

"Look," said Lillian as she pulled out some fabric. "We can use these old lace curtains to make a pretty dust ruffle."

"Do you think they're too white?" wondered Laura.

"We'll dip them in tea to make them ivory," suggested Claudette.

You could almost see the wheels turning in their heads! They decided to paint the room a soft buttery color. A pretty vintage quilt with a pastel print would cover the bed, and an antique crocheted tablecloth could be folded across the end. They had so many ideas!

"Let's meet this weekend to work on the room," suggested Gloria as the others nodded in agreement.

"And as soon as your mother has had time to settle in," offered Laura, "we will have a 'welcome' tea just for her and invite some of the ladies her age who live in the neighborhood and attend the local church."

Suzette was so thankful for all of their help, especially grateful for their willingness to include her mother. The tea society wanted her in their group very much. Age made no difference to them. But knowing that Claire was such a "people person," Suzette did not think it would be long before her mother had so many new friends that she had formed an annex to the tea society.

"Perhaps," mused Suzette, "she will call it the Silver Tea Society!"

SANDY'S TEA SOCIETY DECORATING IDEAS

Here's how the tea society turned Suzette's spare "junk" room
into a cozy haven for Suzette's mother, Claire.

- PLENTY OF PILLOWS: *To make a pretty, restful bed, Ruby made ivory pillow shams with ruffles to support layers of pillows. She added lace ruffles to the open end of old embroidered pillow-cases. She also used embroidered dresser scarves to make more pillows, and even showcased an antique crocheted doily on a pale blue throw pillow.*

- A HEAVENLY HEADBOARD: *Claudette decided to pad the plain headboard on the bed and cover it with a pale yellow and white striped fabric. Then she "tufted" it by tacking the fabric to the headboard and gently sewing large vintage buttons on top of the tacks.*

- WONDERFUL WINDOWS: *Suzette had already found pretty fabric with pink and yellow roses for the room. Laura showed her how to swag the fabric across the tops of the windows and then gather the fullness on either side in place with a little piece of wire and hang it on a nail on each upper corner of the window. Then she let the fabric fall and puddle on the floor on both sides of the window. She attached pretty yellow striped fabric (the same fabric used for the headboard) to cover the nail.*

- SMART STORAGE: *Lillian made a cover for an old cedar chest out of the same floral fabric used for the window coverings. The tea society put the chest at the foot of the bed to give Claire extra storage space.*

- BEAUTIFUL BOOKSHELVES: *Gloria painted a large bookshelf a soft shade of ivory and attached heavy cotton lace to the edges of the shelves. She also painted a rocking chair the same shade of ivory and set it next to a small, round table adorned with a yellow and white striped cloth—ready for Claire's teacup, glasses, and books.*

- FINISHING TOUCHES: *Laura crocheted a soft pink afghan for Claire's rocking chair. Claudette brought in a stack of pretty, empty hatboxes to provide extra storage. The tea society arranged a cozy area under the window for Claire's treadle sewing machine. Ruby created a finishing flourish by hammering four nails into the wall over the bed. She had found four beautiful floral hankies in the cedar chest and had framed each one in a square frame. And Suzette brought in a tea tray and a blue and white china pitcher full of flowers for the table.*

Sandy Lynam Clough

Friendship Tea at Sandy's

I COULD HARDLY WAIT TO SEE them all together—the members of Sandy's Tea Society. Peeking out the parlor window for early arrivals, I saw Ruby coming up the sidewalk with a young woman I had never seen before. I scurried to add another teacup and saucer, plate, and silverware to the table before the ladies reached my front porch. I understood that the tea society had been surprising each other for weeks. Now they were surprising me! Having another guest joining us only increased my expectation for a delightful afternoon.

I scooted to the door and opened it wide before Ruby could ring the bell. Ruby presented her guest, Veronica, as I invited them in and gave them both a heartfelt welcome. Before I could begin to become acquainted with Veronica, five more good friends were at my door.

It was amazing to see how the previous reserve of these ladies had been replaced by an expressive warmth of spirit. They had certainly grown close since that first tea party I had arranged to introduce them to each other!

SANDY'S TEA SOCIETY CAKE

2 cups sugar • 2 cups flour • 1 tsp baking soda
2 tsps cinnamon • 1 tsp instant coffee granules
2 sticks margarine • 4 tsps cocoa
1 cup water • ½ cup buttermilk
2 eggs • 1 tsp vanilla • 1 tsp orange extract

Sift together flour, sugar, baking soda, cinnamon, and coffee. Set aside. In a saucepan, melt margarine. Add cocoa and water and bring to a boil. Pour over flour mixture. Quickly add buttermilk, eggs, vanilla, and orange extract. Mix well. Pour into a greased and floured 9 x 13 baking dish. Bake at 400 degrees for 20 minutes or when top springs back when touched.

ICING

1 stick margarine, melted • 4 tbsps cocoa
6 tbsps buttermilk • 1 tbsp vanilla
¼ tsp instant coffee granules
1 tsp orange extract • 1 box powdered sugar
1 cup chopped pecans or slivered almonds

In a large saucepan, combine margarine, cocoa, and buttermilk. Bring to a boil. Stir in vanilla, coffee, and orange extract. Reduce heat. Add powdered sugar and nuts. Mix well. Pour over cake.

Wanting to make Veronica feel comfortable and included, I explained to her what I had asked the ladies to do at this tea party. Because they had been having tea together for the past season, I had asked them to bring something today that symbolized Sandy's Tea Society or what they had learned about friendship by sharing tea with kindred hearts. Veronica seemed genuinely at ease and not surprised at all. She joined the beautiful circle of friendship gathered around my table. Over the warm teacups, the ladies began to share their hearts.

Lillian reached into her pocket and pulled out a thimble. "My mother told me that choosing good friends could protect me from many of the pricks of life, much like a thimble protects my finger. Good friends also cushion the unavoidable pricks of life."

I was hoping that Veronica wouldn't feel left out as these ladies described how they felt about their friendship.

Suzette pulled an envelope out of her purse and shook it so that they could hear the seeds rattle. "Having friends is like growing in the midst of a flower garden instead of being planted alone in a pot."

Claudette gently displayed an old lace hankie made of lace strips sewn together. "All the pieces are different and pretty on their own, but together they are more beautiful and useful. Every piece is important."

Laura slipped into the kitchen and brought the cake she had created. "This is Sandy's Tea Society's official cake. Just as the ingredients of this cake are made more appealing when they are mixed together, what we all bring to the group increases our joy. Soft-spoken Claudette is the flour. Lillian reminds me of the sweetness of the sugar. Gloria is the freshness of the fruit. Ruby's creative flavor is the cinnamon. And Suzette's cheerful caring is the salt that preserves."

"What are you?" I wondered aloud.

"I want to be the oil that helps hold it all together."

"What is the chocolate for?" I asked.

"Our well-being," Laura replied with a smile.

Everyone had now shared except Ruby.

Make new friends, but keep the old,

Those are silver, these are gold.

I turned to her and asked, "Ruby, what did you bring that symbolizes the tea society for you?"

"I brought Veronica, a new friend for all of us," Ruby smiled. "That's what Sandy's Tea Society is all about—joining kindred hearts with a cup of friendship." With that, she gave each lady in the room a pretty card along with a decorative pin of a teacup, saucer, and spoon. On the card was written the verse—*Make new friends, but keep the old, those are silver, these are gold.*

As each lady looked at her pin and then smiled at Veronica, I could see another idea brewing in their creative minds—a tea party to properly welcome the newest member of Sandy's Tea Society! These ladies were already thinking of acts of kindness that might add to the joys of her life, for she had already added to their joy by becoming a new friend.

When I first introduced Gloria, Suzette, Lillian, Laura, Claudette, and Ruby to you, they had a need. Now they are rich in friendships, for they have both silver and gold. They are very rich ladies indeed.

POSTSCRIPT

"FRIENDSHIP IS A GIFT WE GET TO open over and over again with each new visit. Because you brought us together, we brought you a gift today." From behind her back, Ruby produced a lovely drawing of the tea society at Gloria's tea party. She had even drawn herself in the group. And in a little oval cut in the mat around the picture was a piece of Claudette's broken teacup. On the brass title plate attached to the frame was inscribed, "Kindred Hearts—Sandy's Tea Society."

I hung it in my tearoom, and there it hangs today, where I shall treasure it always.

Have you ever thought of forming your own tea society? Imagine the delightful friends waiting to be "in the picture"—with you! If you would like more ideas for joining kindred hearts with a cup of friendship, please write.

SANDY'S TEA SOCIETY
P.O. Box 85
Powder Springs, GA
30127-0085

Or we invite you to join us on the internet at:

www.sandysteasociety.com

There is a tea party waiting there for you!